RESPECTING OTHERS

By Steffi Cavell-Clarke

Our Values

©2017
Book Life
King's Lynn
Norfolk PE30 4LS

ISBN: 978-1-78637-114-0

All rights reserved
Printed in Malaysia

Written by:
Steffi Cavell-Clarke

Edited by:
Grace Jones

Designed by:
Natalie Carr

A catalogue record for this book
is available from the British Library.

CONTENTS

Words that look like **this** can be found in the glossary on page 24.

WHAT ARE OUR VALUES?

Values are ideas and beliefs that help us to work and live together in a **community**. Values teach us how to behave and how we should **respect** each other and ourselves.

4

Respecting others

Understanding different faiths

Making your own choices

Being responsible

Our Values

Helping others

Sharing your ideas

Respecting the law

Listening to others

5

BEING RESPECTFUL

Being respectful means that we behave in a way that shows the people around us that we care about their feelings and rights. We can be respectful by treating others the way we would like to be treated.

We can show respect towards other people by being polite, kind and honest. One of the ways we can be polite is by saying "thank you" when someone does something kind for us.

"May I have an ice cream, please?"

To show respect when she asks for something, Alice always says "please".

7

WHY IS IT IMPORTANT?

Being respectful to each other allows us to work and live together happily within a community. It also means that we can make friends more easily and show kindness towards our family members.

It is important that we show each other respect because it means that we care about other people's feelings. It is also important that other people respect our feelings too.

How are you feeling?

Worried

Sad

Happy

Angry

RESPECTING THE LAW

Laws are rules that people in our community should always try to follow. Laws help to keep us safe and help us to make the right choices.

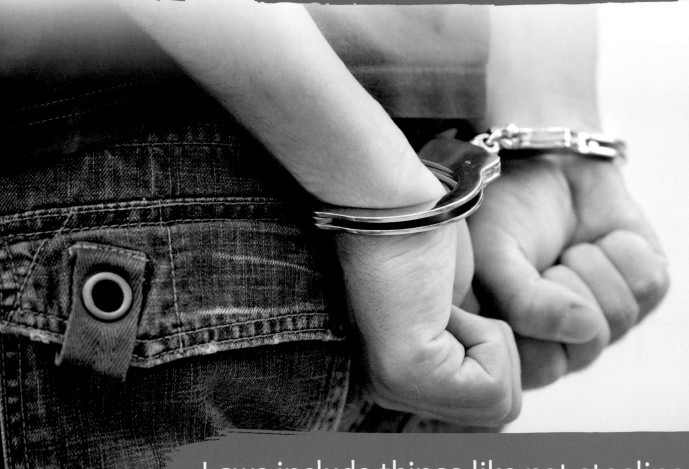

Laws include things like not stealing or harming other people. We must not break the law. If we do, we are carrying out a **crime**.

Police Officer

Police officers are people who help everyone in our communities. They have a very important job to do; they make sure that we follow the law and try to keep us safe from harm.

RESPECTING OTHER RELIGIONS

Choosing what to believe in is an important part of your **freedom**. There are many religions that people can choose to follow and they can all be very different. We must always respect other people's religions, no matter how different they might be.

If you feel confused about someone else's religion, you can ask thoughtful questions to help you to understand more about it. You should always respect someone else's beliefs, whether you agree with them or not.

RESPECTING OURSELVES

It is very important that we respect ourselves; this is called self-respect. To show self-respect, we look after our bodies and try our best to have good relationships with our friends and families.

Staying healthy and keeping clean also shows that you have respect for yourself. Keeping clean is called **personal hygiene**.

Sarah brushes her teeth and her hair every morning so she can feel good about herself.

LISTENING TO OTHERS

It is important to listen to other people because it will help you to understand what they might be thinking and how they might be feeling. Listening to others is one way of showing respect towards them.

Thomas likes to ask his mum how she is feeling because he cares about her. He listens to what she says and it makes them both feel happy. It also shows that they have a good relationship.

RESPECTING OTHERS AT SCHOOL

We must show respect towards our teachers and other people at our school. Our teachers want to teach us lots of new things, so it is important that we are quiet when they are speaking and listen carefully.

Charlotte and her friends are very quiet when they visit the library. They respect other people's need to read without being **disrupted**. Being quiet also lets them focus on choosing the right book.

RESPECTING OTHERS AT HOME

We must always try to show respect to the people we live with at home. We can show them respect by doing helpful things and being polite to one another.

Adam respects his parents and likes to help them to do jobs around the house. He knows that making his bed and washing the dishes will help his parents and show them that he cares about them.

21

MAKING A DIFFERENCE

We can respect the **environment** by putting our rubbish in a rubbish bin. We can recycle paper, cardboard and plastic so it can be reused.

Remember never to throw litter on the ground.

Think of all the ways you can be a good friend.

Share

Be Kind

Be Helpful

Give it a go today, you could make a new friend!

Say "Hello"

Be Polite

Listen

23

GLOSSARY

community	a group of people living in the same area who share similar values
crime	doing something that breaks the law
disrupted	something that has been interrupted
environment	your surroundings
freedom	being allowed to do something
law	rules that a community has to follow
personal hygiene	keeping yourself clean
respect	feeling that something or someone is important
responsible	to be trusted to do the right thing

INDEX

PHOTOCREDITS

Photocredits: Abbreviations: l – left, r –right, b – bottom, t – top, c-centre, m – middle.
2-3 Monkey Business Images. 4 – Rawpixel.com. 5tl – Monkey Business Images. 5tm – Tom Wang. 5tr – Yuliya Evstratenko. 5ml – Andresr. 5mr – ISchmidt. 5bl – Lucian Milasan. 5bm – Pressmaster. 5br – Luis Molinero. 6 -Sergey Novikov. 7 - Maryna Pleshkun. 8 - Pressmaster. 9ml - supparsorn. 9mr - Anastasiia Markus. 9br - Maria Symchych. 9tm - Bosnian 10 - Alexander Raths. 11 - 1000 Words. 12 - YanLev. 13 - InesBazdar. 14 - Mitskevich Uladzimir. 15 - Oksana Kuzmina. 16 - Monkey Business Images. 17 - Angela Luchianiuc. 18 - wavebreakmedia. 19 - Tatiana Bobkova. 20 - Kinga. 21 - Oksana Kuzmina. 22 - wavebreakmedia. 23tl - ISchmidt. 23tm - Alinute Silzeviciute. 23tr - ISchmidt. 23bl - Syda Productions. 23bm - Pressmaster. 23br - naluwan.
Images are courtesy of Shutterstock.com. With thanks to Getty Images, Thinkstock Photo and iStockphoto.